TIMELESS KITCHENS

BETA-PLUS

TIMELESS KITCHENS
originally published in Dutch and French
TIJDLOZE KEUKENS/CUISINES INTEMPORELLES

PUBLISHER

BETA-PLUS sa
Termuninck 3
7850 Enghien
Belgium
Tel : +32 (0)2 395 90 20
Fax : +32 (0)2 395 90 21
Website: www.betaplus.com
E-mail: betaplus@skynet.be

PHOTOGRAPHY

Jo Pauwels a.o. (photography credits p. 216)

LAYOUT

POLYDEM sprl
Nathalie Binart

TRANSLATION

Alexia Aughuet (Dutch to French)
Yvonne Lim and Serena Narain (French to English)

August 2005
ISBN: 907-721-338-4

LEFT

This kitchen was created by Fahrenheit.

Interior design by Dominique d'Ursel (Les Petites Heures du Matin).

NEXT

Kitchen

designed by

Francis Van Damme.

CONTENTS

PREFACE

Long recognised as the heart of the home, kitchens are a true reflection of an owner's personality. To give you an insight into various kitchen designs realised by renowned architects and interior designers, this publication presents over 20 beautiful kitchens that reflect quality and durability.

'Individuality' remains as the common trait of all the works featured in this edition. Each kitchen presented is unique and has been built according to the client's briefs. Only current yet timeless projects of natural, good quality and durable materials are included.

Respect for craft-design is as important as the functionality of the kitchens presented in this issue; the furnaces are selected from a series of top-of-the-range and exclusive cookers. Together with the most recent electric household apparatuses, they are integrated ingeniously into a harmonious whole.

These works serve as a source of inspirations for those who wish to transform their kitchen into a welcoming and timeless piece.

www.betaplus.com

NEXT
Kitchen designed by 'Moris Groupe'

CHAPTER 1

ACHIEVEMENTS OF KITCHEN CREATORS

DE MENAGERIE : A CHEERFUL AND MORE LIVABLE MINIMALISM

In 1997, Luc Lormans set up an enterprise that has in a few years, made a name in the up-market kitchen fabricator industry in Belgium, known as De Menagerie.

In the showroom at Alost, visitors impregnate instantly to an atmosphere that is drawn into these kitchens: country-style projects that refine a cheerful and finer livable minimalism.

The kitchens of De Menagerie have an absence of unnecessary embellishments of style, instead they emphasise on durability, natural materials and accentuate on right proportions with the perfect finish. Sober and timeless, these works integrate perfectly into contemporary classical interiors, which turn out as good as new.

LEFT AND ABOVE:
De Menagerie completed this kitchen in glossed oak with a Lacanche cooker and an island counter constituting a sink and a worktop in a new construction. The hood, in stainless steel custom-made to size, has an external engine and is supported on consoles made of blue stone. Moroccan slates are found on the wall. The smoothened stone countertops in Buxy Ash are by Philippe Van Den Weghe. Mixer taps from Volevatch (near the window) and from Lefroy Brooks (at the island).

P. 18 TO 21
The kitchen, built by architect Bart Moors in a Limbourgeoise old farm that constitutes authentic elements, has a contemporary style. It is made of painted oak with a high-end cooker from Viking. The hood is ingeniously installed and slots nicely into a niche. The spoon shelf is fabricated to measure by De Menagerie. The petits blancs white tiles from Makkum authentic have been chosen to cover the wall above the stove. Floor and other surfaces are finished with blue stone. Mixer taps are from Dornbracht; handles are in spick and span mat version. The 'cozy corner' is relocated to a very narrow and deep space (approx. 2.3 x 6m). The huge wall cupboard could contain numerous utensils with in-built natural stone work tops. Existing exposed beams are recognised and integrated into the new kitchen design.

LEFT AND ABOVE:

Within this ancient villa situated in magnificent surroundings of vast greenery is an entirely new kitchen installed in painted solid oak. The stove and wine cellar (on the left of the door) are from Viking. The Buxy worktop is by Philippe Van Den Weghe. One can appreciate the Moroccan slates above the stove. Mixer taps from 'Profi' series by Dornbracht.

The oak kitchen cabinets in this classical villa have been colour-stained. The objective of the transformation is to accentuate the horizontality of the space up to the extent of the wood structure. The countertops are in Buxy Ash with a heating system harmoniously concealed within the island counter.

The handles in moulded iron accentuate the horizontality of the kitchen.

All appliances are from Gaggenau, mixer taps are from Dornbracht.

An American fridge in aluminium finish from Gaggenau.

Perfect finish assured by De Menagerie:

A constant passion for perfection.

Kitchen in oak veneer, countertop and huge sink are in Bleu de Tavel natural stone.
Mixer taps from Volevatch.

Left:

This kitchen, equipped with a Gaggenau stove, is made of painted old oak. The low walls define the cooking zone.
Countertop in Buxy finely shaded; Moroccan slates on the wall. Similarly, the accessories are custom-made
to size.

LEFT AND ABOVE:

A humane minimalism rules over this ancient house with a Gantese owner, which is designed in American walnut wood and shutters in solid wood. The countertop in Belfast Extra granite (Noir de Marlin) has a smooth finish. Mixer taps are from the 'Meta' series by Dornbracht. Ceramic floor tiles are from Cotta d'Este.

FAHRENHEIT: TOP-OF-THE-RANGE BRUSSELS KITCHENS SPECIALIST

Fahrenheit Home Chef, established in Brussels, is the creator of kitchens and the distributor of exclusive kitchen accessories. All the appliances distributed by Fahrenheit display a professional seal, but are designed only for private use. At the end of 2003, the Brussels kitchen maker presented a kitchen counter 90 centimetres wide: the project was signed on by Fahrenheit and created in Belgium, following the strictest of standards.

The kitchens of Fahrenheit emphasise on durability and a perfect completion. The three projects shown in this article are the characteristics of research quality.

LEFT, OPPOSITE AND NEXT

This kitchen was created by Fahrenheit for an old house belonging to Ambassadors in the 20s.

The sink is surrounded by cabinets covered in oak strips. The sink, countertop and the wall are finished off with "Pierre d'Aubergine", an Italian sandstone exclusively imported by Fahrenheit. The valves and fittings are from KWC, tap is "Domo Gastro" with a shower head that facilitates the cleaning of deep and hollow plates. Pans and stoves are from Roesle. A Lacanche (model "Fougeot") cooker is integrated onto a bar counter with matching stools. Fahrenheit has designed the entire block.

Refrigerator is from Viking.

The hood is in a 'glasshouse' style fabricated in ancient glass and oak wood, and is equipped with halogen spotlights that are a specialty of Fahrenheit.

Interior design by Dominique d'Ursel (Les Petites Heures du Matin).

Aesthetics and functionality preside harmoniously over the concept of this kitchen by designer Robert Degroeve. The furniture is in painted dark maroon MDF board and the countertop is in "Pierre d'Aubergine". Fahrenheit designed the hood and stools.

P. 34-35

In this house that belongs to a famous American fashion stylist located at Place Stephanie in Brussels, Fahrenheit transformed the kitchen to a true family room with a large table, a bar with a cooking zone, ample working space and a zone reserved for crockery. All the furniture was fabricated from old oak and the countertop is in blue stone. The wall is covered with Moroccan slates from Agnès Emery (Noir d'Ivoire). On the left of the photo shows a "bottom-mount" refrigerator from Amana's 'Pro Line' series. Tap is from Volevatch; food processor is from KitchenAid. The cabinets are in oak with wrought iron criss-cross patterned windows.

TACK: THE PASSION
OF PERFECTION

During the last years, Frank Tack has earned himself a reputation as a creator and fabricator of up-market kitchens with a prevailing and timeless style.

The dialogues with the client are paramount: Tack's wish is to take into account functionality as well as aesthetics. From conceptual stage to realisation, the company professionally ensures the follow-up of projects, thanks to testing experts and the perfect execution of works in their proper workshops.

LEFT AND ABOVE
Kitchen is in natural oak.
Sink and wall coating are
finished in Jura marble.
Handles are in massive
iron.
To the extreme left is a
cabinet in segments; to
the right of the
integrated door (that
consists of a cold room)
are 2 cupboards with
glass panels. A very
spacious island counter
constitutes a worktop
with a sink.
The hood is perfectly
integrated with its motor
located in the garage.

NEXT
In this holiday house located at the Belgian littoral, Tack has positioned a kitchen in American oak decorated with natural Buxy stone countertop. Above the island is the hood with integrated lighting. The dining table and its cubic base are likewise fabricated from American oak.

Despite a strong growth, Tack has preserved a strong family tradition: Frank Tack and his wife take personal care of all contacts with the clients. Flexibility and personal contacts are thus their essential assets.

Tack deliberately chooses durable materials and dignified materials for the craft-design. All details are thought through and realised carefully to achieve comfort: the kitchens featured in this publication emphasise quality works.

LEFT AND ABOVE

This kitchen in oak is painted in olive and grey tints. Jura blue stone is chosen for the countertop. The stove is from Lacanche.

The door is framed and integrated into the full height cabinet against the wall.

NEXT

A timeless kitchen with a Westahl stove. A large sink in blue stone is fabricated in Tack's workshop. The oak table is custom-made and whitewashed. Certain details reveal a refinement: rusted handles, adapted lighting, Moroccan slates on wall, etc.

This kitchen cabinet, equipped with an IIve stove, is built in ivory oak. A functional island and the worktop are
covered with grey Buxy. Subway tiling covers the wall above the stove. A porcelain vat is integrated in this project.

BOURGONDISCH KRUIS: FROM OLD STONE TO THE COMPLETE INSTALLATION OF KITCHENS

It has been over ten years that Bourgondisch Kruis was launched into the trade of rustic construction materials and has become the principal reference in the industry of Bourgogne sandstone and reprocessed oak treatment.

A western Flanders enterprise driven in a dynamic way by Kurt Deplancke and Andy Vanhoutte, Bourgondisch Kruis knows indeed how to integrate these construction materials into prestigious residential projects.

An ATAG refrigerator with water and ice dispenser is integrated into a wall covered in Bourgogne stone.

LEFT AND ABOVE

In an old villa, built in local stone, Bourgondisch Kruis has designed a kitchen, a dining room and a back kitchen.

The ground, countertop and wall linings are in Bourgogne sandstone. The cabinets are fabricated from an old wall cupboard in glossed oak.

Cooker by Lacanche.

Kitchens constitute the principal specialty of the Harelbeke enterprise, which has its own joinery workshop where a team of carpenters completes a perfect made-to-measure work in oak panels. At the stone workshop, calcareous stones from Bourgogne and blue stones are transformed into exclusive elements that find their proper place in the kitchen (work tops, ground and wall linings, as well as elegant sinks). Either the client proposes his very own ideas or the internal team of kitchen specialists will put forward a refined and extremely personal kitchen project.

The old construction materials Bourgondisch Kruis integrated into these projects reveal a secular charm.

The works illustrated in these pages witness a high degree of functionality and good control of details, style and class.

LEFT AND ABOVE

A kitchen recently renovated in a 70's dwelling.

Several small pieces of kitchen furniture are amalgamated into one large whole. The kitchen cupboards are fabricated from ancient oak boards in natural finish.

Right in the center of the kitchen features
a 1.3m x 2.3m professional cooker from Molteni.
The dream hood equipped with an external motor
has similarly been delivered by Bourgondisch
Kruis. A large ancient double sink in blue stone
has been incorporated in this kitchen.

This kitchen in this villa of the 50's has been transformed by Bourgondisch Kruis into a harmonious whole composed of flagstones from Bourgogne, painted old oak panels, wall tiling, countertops and a recently fabricated block (photo on the right) in limestone from Bourgogne.

ANTIQUES & DESIGN:
FROM KITCHEN TO COMPLETE INSTALLATION

Antiques & Design is an internationally renowned restoration enterprise that executes complete interior fit-out with ancient materials. In a quarter of a century, this enterprise has made a name in the renovation industry and in the industry of old furniture restoration, mainly in pinewood.

Kitchens constitute one of the enterprise's principal activities. All the kitchens created by Antiques & Design are entirely custom-made to size or according to clients' wishes: with or without a cooking island, wicker baskets, bottles carrier, refrigerators, embedded elements, supplementary arrangements, etc. All the large electric household appliances are carefully integrated in a timeless and prestigious concept.

The follow-up of all the projects is personally ensured by the two managers, Karel Van Beek and Gert Verhees. They respect precise working methods: First, overall concept and style are discussed with the client, thereafter the budget is fixed and outlines are set up.

LEFT, ABOVE AND NEXT

This spacious kitchen in patinated solid larch is part of a complete interior renovation in a 1950's villa by Antiques & Design.

A block of varnish beech and a Boretti cooker are incorporated into the small cooking island.

Worktops are constructed in black Jasberg granite; the grounds are covered with Carrara white marble with Jasberg cabochons.

Ultimately the drawings and plans are formulated into three-dimensional visualisations on a computer for the client to imagine his kitchen better. Finally the entrepreneur, the electricians, the plumbers and relevant experts came into the scene accordingly. These works are also coordinated by the Geel enterprise.

This global approach is greatly appreciated by the client: a common trust is formed which adds to the flexibility and professionalism of Antiques & Design in a more than satisfactory result. The kitchen is very often only the first stage in the realisation of a complete interior project whereby Antiques & Design applies the same quality systematically.

Two classical refrigerators are integrated harmoniously into this kitchen project.

LEFT AND ABOVE

All the kitchens created by Antiques & Design are realised according to clients' wishes: a perfection of made-to-measure works.

Very durable materials are used in this kitchen: the floor is covered with stone from Bourgogne, the interior door is in solid mass pine from the Switzerland suburbs, worktops are in Carrara marble and selective solid maple wood, authentic Dutch petits blancs white tiles adorn the walls while the drawers are in solid beech.

The gas cooker from Morice has a width of 180cm and contains 2 furnaces.

MARK WILKINSON: TRADITIONAL PURE ENGLISH UP-MARKET KITCHENS

Mark Wilkinson and his wife, Cynthia, left a furniture factory in 1981 that they had set up with several friends in 1976 to open their very own enterprise: Mark Wilkinson Furniture. In a little more than 20 years, this English furniture manufacturer has become one of the most renowned kitchen fabricators in the international scene and has eight showrooms in the United Kingdom, subsequently starting establishments in Paris, Moscow, Dublin, United States and in Antwerp after 1993.
A true trendsetter, Mark Wilkinson has, over 20 years, developed the concepts of timeless kitchens in different styles and executed in oak, cherry wood, ash wood, maple, walnut or manually-painted poplar.

Valves and fittings from Perrin & Rowe; Sink from Shaws.

The controls for the hood are cleverly dissimulated in the small cupboard with ceramic and antique brass.

LEFT

This Mark Wilkinson kitchen inspired from the suburbs was conceived by Annemiek Hamelink for a recently constructed traditional countryside house. The kitchen was pieced together in a professional way by its team of craftsmen. The cooker with a fryer is from "Chambertin", Lacanche. The floor is in natural Travertino Noce stone and the kitchen Platinium Range English wall tiling is from Portazul, a tile enterprise that Mark Wilkinson usually works with.

Interiors of the cupboard are painted on-site in ash wood with ash wood plating. Worktops are in Pietra Serena marble with a softened finish. The refrigerator and steam furnace from Imperial are integrated in the cupboards that also comprise a custom-made food cabinet.

NEXT
All the Mark Wilkinson kitchens are fabricated in England and executed according to the client's requirements.

Mark Wilkinson's exclusive showroom situated in Vlaamsekaai, Antwerp was inaugurated in May 2001 by Ivo de Groot and Annemiek Hamelink. Annemiek manages the showroom. She is an industrial conceptualist who adds sensibility and style to her knowledge of craft-design techniques and materials. In these projects, the furniture fabricated in England responds to the taste and criteria from the Flemish region without making the least inaccuracy with the patented original model. Annemiek Hamelink's style is sombre and practical; her approach, however, has always pushed forward clients' wishes and their desired lifestyles: Furniture, style, colours, lighting, floor, wall coverings, etc are all coordinated.

Mark Wilkinson also offers a choice between several exclusive brands of cooker and electrical household appliances that are well-integrated into prestigious kitchens in the market – Lacanche, Aga, Viking, Wolf, SubZero, Miele, Imperial, etc.

The showroom in Antwerp offers the visitors, in addition to kitchens, a library, an office and a small bathroom. In fact, Mark Wilkinson is not only an originator and fabricator of kitchen, the company also proposes complete interior renovation projects to the client.

LEFT AND THIS PAGE
Mark Wilkinson's "Cooks" kitchen exists since the creation of the enterprise in 1981. The popular concept has been able to meet the general requirements and has been the base of contemporary kitchen installations for more than 20 years. Worktop of this kitchen equipped with an Aga cook is in softened Jasberg granite with a "parrot's nozzle" edge. Furniture is fabricated in poplar for its stability; Cupboard interiors are in ash wood and ash wood laminates. A refrigerator and a traditional freezer are integrated into a large cabinet whereas next to the cabinet, is a pantry which can be organized in whichever way the client wishes.

OBUMEX: THE ABSOLUTE THEORETICAL REQUIREMENT

Obumex is concerned in answering clients' very personal requirements and taking sufficient time to communicate with them (like soul mates) in order to understand their needs. Obumex takes the necessary time to share with the client its expertise, knowledge, experiences and its savoir-faire. In this manner, each project, whether it is a whole construction or interior project, is realised with the concern for perfection with the smallest details. The touch of audacity, quality of execution, aesthetics, a durable label and excellent service, are the applicable words to describe the works of Obumex. Each time it has a renewed passion, whatever the style is.

In this article, each work witnesses a unique style, which Obumex has realised from its dialogues with the client. These are projects that display a degree of upper class, luxury, as well as a practical conception of space. Aesthetics is not the only factor; the cook has to enjoy and feel the pleasure of using the kitchen.

LEFT AND ABOVE
A laquer kitchen with a centre island where the Gaggenau appliances are integrated. The shelves in brown tint are from Buxy Brun and the cabinets in tinted Sycamore wood above the sink soften stiffness of the lines.

Obumex has a team of passionate collaborators who is able to set up, in theory, the absolute requirement. The expertise in the enterprise is not limited and as such, the result is as proper and neatly done as it appears. This theory is worth as much for the realisation of kitchen projects as for the complete interior fit-out or for a workplace within the quality of life. For instance, from the total installation of a bathroom, library or a personalised pharmacy, as well as conference rooms and offices.

The furniture is from the unique collections of Promemoria, Christian Liaigre and B&B Italia, which are in tune with the style of Obumex.

LEFT AND ABOVE
The mixture of blue stone, tinted sycamore wood and stainless steel produces a graphical play of surfaces and volumes. A Tara Classic tap furnishes the custom-made sink.

The station between the kitchen and the dining room is where the plates are stored in glass cabinets. The walls are painted in a subtle greenish tint, which accentuates harmony between the garden, kitchen and the dining room.

THE SAVOIR-FAIRE CRAFT-DESIGN INDUSTRY OF COUSAERT - VAN DER DONCKT

Cousaert – Van der Donckt takes care of the conception and the realisation of kitchen fabrication, emphasising on the craft-design and artistry custom-made to the client's requirements. This enterprise from Kluisbergen (Ardennes flamandes), founded in 1992 by Dirk Cousaert, has a clear preference for restoration of materials and the ancestral craftsmanship techniques. In most of the kitchens done by Cousaert – Van der Donckt, there is a combination of ancient blue stone solid sink, old elements in oak wood and antique taps. The coherent implementation of ancestral principles (tenon and mortise, swallow's tail) confers the kitchens with a distinct and timeless seal.

If you have a preference for country-style kitchens which carry the attributes of time, make an appointment at the showroom situated next to the workshops of Cousaert – Van der Donckt, which exhibits a diverse installation of ideas like an "a la carte" menu whereby the client's requirements are chosen and observed.

NEXT
In this grand country villa, Cousaert – Van der Donckt has created a distinguished kitchen with a mixture of old and new. The countertop in blue stone has been manually polished and softened in the Cousaert workshops. Similarly the base is in blue stone. Wall tiles are Moroccan slates. The small window in wrought iron offers a view towards the back of the kitchen.

LEFT AND ABOVE
In this kitchen project, ancient oak planks, a restored large sink and new oak wood elements form a harmonious whole.

The details show different handles on the kitchen furniture. Blue stone countertop was engraved in the workshops of Cousaert – Van der Donckt.

A panel in rare Noir de Mazy stone was restored and utilised as a worktop and sink.

In an ancient house, the floor tiles and original chimney were conserved.

Cousaert – Van der Donckt has imagined a kitchen project that perfectly frames an impression of living, which rules this house.

This summer kitchen was reinforced with waterproof adhesive and exhibits an assembly of tenon and mortise with blue stone base to make it more durable. The blue stone and other elements in oak wood were assembled to allow for better water discharge.

Cousaert – Van der Donckt has furthermore envisaged a barbeque pit for this summer kitchen that could be completely modular depending on the client's requirement.

Cousaert – Van der Donckt has an estimated stock of 150 ancient large sink of all dimensions.

A bold contrast: carcass in bleached oak with countertop and sink in secular Noir de Mazy stone.

THE CRAFT-DESIGN KITCHENS OF "IL ETAIT UNE FOIS.."

In 1996, Anne De Visscher, together with her husband Eric Meert, opened a unique trade in Ixelles, Bruxelles that specialises in the conception and fabrication of craft-design kitchens and bathrooms. It is known as "Il était une fois..".

All the kitchens from this Brussels enterprise feature timeless characteristics and are fabricated according to strict standards of high quality. They are made-to-measure and adapted to meet their clients' ways of living. The client's requirement form the basis of each project.

Left and above

The "Cottage" kitchen of "Il était une fois.." in a renovated dwelling. The furniture is made of high-quality water resistant MDF boards. The countertop is in timber from Afzelia; portugese cement squares in bright yellow and aubergine tones. The mauve colour wall (behind the shelves) comes from a mixture of two Flamingo colours: Digue and Grand Cru. The cooker is from Viking; tap is from Pendragon.

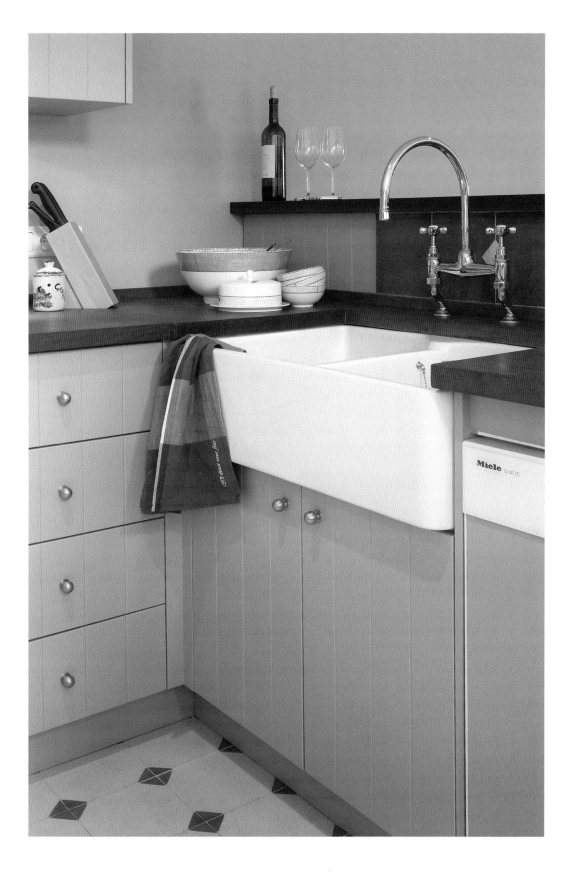

"L'Ouest":
a contemporary kitchen
concept with countertop
in Afzelia timber, Campo
cement square tiles for
the floor (with cabochons
anthracite) and
contrasting wall tiles.
The cabinets were
painted with paint from
Farrow & Ball (Summer
House).

Double-sink is from
Timbre d'Office, with tap
from Pendragon. The
button-like handles of the
cabinet doors are in
brushed stainless steel.

The furniture was painted after installation, which allows high flexibility in choice and utilisation of colours.

Works shown on these pages are very good examples.

The range from "Il était une fois.." concentrates around three cardinals points (North, South and West) and a cottage style. It would include three other styles for the kitchen design starting from 2004.

Although they specialise in the conception of kitchens, "Il était une fois.." also offers a complete service in restoration and renovation projects, for instance, electrical and sanitary installations, and restoration of floors, joinery and paintings.

It has developed into a multi-purpose and flexible company whose reputation largely exceeds the cradle of Brussels. "Il était une fois.." has by now realised a multitude of projects in other countries.

LEFT AND ABOVE

South: A contemporary kitchen inspired from the southerner in a renovated house in Brussels. Similarly, the Afzelian timber was used for the worktop. In this project, "Il était une fois.." associated two colours that they invented, "Saut du lit" and "Peche".

North: This renovated kitchen has a northern ambience where the original pine floor is conserved.

The furniture is in Flamingo "Golden Champagne" and walls are in Flamingo "Bord de Seine".

The Portugese cement tiles create a warm atmosphere.

THE DURABLE KITCHEN
OF COUNTRY COOKING

For many years, Country Cooking has been the exclusive import company of kitchens from the legendary Nobel and Imperial. In regular intervals, the Gantese establishment organises exhibitions and workshops of these up-market cookers.

Recently, Juanita Pascual, founder and spiritual Mother of the industry, decided to add a series of kitchens in its distribution activities.

The vision of Country Cooking starts from the base concept that a kitchen is decorated like any other rooms in the house. A kitchen need not be uniquely a functional space. Thanks to the correct association of furniture and colors, and to sensible integration of appliances, the kitchen can be transformed into a very pleasant living space.

LEFT AND ABOVE

In this new showroom in Knokke, Country Cooking, the import company of English cast iron cooker Nobel and Imperial, presents a spread of kitchens that tallies perfectly with the country-style robustness of these cookers. All the kitchens are fabricated in solid wood and entirely assembled together in an "à la carte" manner as according to the requirements of the client.

All the cupboards created by Country
Cooking are fabricated in an artisanal
manner and respect ancestral techniques.

The quality precedes: all furniture is created in essences of solid wood (oak, pine or beech) in a totally artisanal manner. The kitchens thus reflect the characteristics of durability and solidness. The choice of materials and the finishes of each kitchen elements are similarly essential.

In these projects, Juanita Pasual takes inspirations from Portugese cloister furniture from the 15th century, which is enriched with a mix of Victorian influences, rectilinear look and the functionality from the style of Shaker.

In addition to its series of furniture, Country Cooking has launched a range of poetic colours inspired from nature and art of living this year.

PAUL VAN DE KOOI:
EXCLUSIVE KITCHENS SERVED "À LA CARTE"

Paul van de Kooi creates and realises exclusive kitchens entirely fabricated from clients' desires in quality materials with an absolute high degree of finish.

Kitchens of Paul van de Kooi are fabricated in a totally artisanal manner and are so good that all the clients' desires can be included in the design. The client can also visit the workshops situated next to the showroom and the conception workshop if he or she wishes.

LEFT AND ABOVE

Paul van de Kooi has placed this cream-colored kitchen in a country house which is located in an idyllic environment. The worktops (4cm thick) are created in Soft Ubatuba granite. The chimney was constructed in ancient petits blancs whites tiles with motifs from Piet Jonker. The valves and fittings are from Dornbracht (Tara Classic). Household electrical appliances are from Imperial. The handles on the cabinet doors are in porcelain.

The private kitchen of Piet Jonker, an "antique dealer on construction materials", whom Paul van de Kooi collaborates regularly with, is in painted solid oak. The custom-made stools have the same finish.

The countertop in blue stone has a thickness of 6cm. "Double Stratos" hood is from Guttman; handles are from RVS.

This kitchen installed in a Paul van de Kooi showroom in Amersfoort, was fabricated from high quality painted MDF board washed in warm yellowish tint. The countertop (6cm thick) is made of terrazzo, an extremely durable material and is installed on site.

Kitchen appliances are from Imperial and Gaggenau. The American refrigerator is from General Electric, and above it is a very practical custom-made wine rack.

Paul van de Kooi has custom-made the table in ancient French oak.

In its showroom, Paul van de Kooi exhibits, within 2-storeys, some 30 kitchens of good proportions, appropriately staged and displayed. All the models displayed have gained enormous success and popularity among the visitors. However, no project is restricted from being "individualised". The clients can choose their requirements like an "à la carte" style of ordering their banquet to form their very own personalised kitchen.

Paul van de Kooi assures the coordination of the entire operation: first the design of custom-fit cabinets, and thereafter the integration of cooker and household electrical appliances. The client has the choice of several splendid up-market cookers: Lacanche, La Cornue, Aga, Boretti, Imperial, etc.

In this article, Paul van de Kooi reveals four kitchen projects: other examples of creative achievements are presented in the enterprise's entirely new site.

Handles are from Rein Tupker,
a Soest inventor.

A beech wood cutlery drawer is visible
behind the glass panel.

LEFT

This present kitchen in a restored farm has an island counter with stainless steel carcass. On the island countertop, a glass panel reveals the beech wood cutlery drawer underneath. The stainless steel sink is embedded and incorporated in the framework. The contrast created by handles of raw steel sheet is very striking.

The kitchen walls are in solid oak painted in grey. The "Lamproom" lights are from Farrow & Ball.

The 150cm long cooker is from Boretti.

THE KITCHENS OF FLAMANT HOME INTERIORS: CURRENT YET TIMELESS

Flamant Home Interiors is a Belgium enterprise that has, in a short time, become an international reference in the domain of interior decorations.

Flamant owes its success primarily to the concept of home decoration stores that the family enterprise launched on prestigious commercial streets in Brussels, Antwerp, Knokke-le-Zoute, Ghent, Liège, Hasselt, Paris, Lille, Breda, Hambourg, etc.

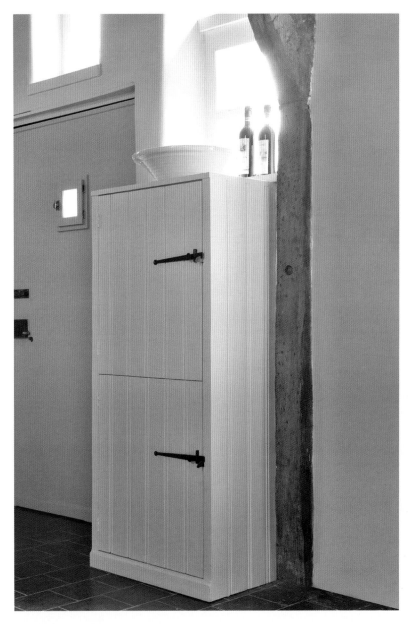

LEFT, ABOVE AND NEXT

This model of kitchen from Flamant known as "Long Island" is painted in "Grey Pepper" colour from Flamant. Cooker is from Aga. The worktop (3cm thick) is fabricated from Belgian blue stone. The chairs from Dauphine and Whatnot, both in natural oak, are from the Flamant collection.

All the items in these stores are entirely designed as an actual living space with all the necessary accessories.

These stores form a beautiful share of a kitchen and in Flamant's philosophy, the kitchen is seen as the heart of a house.

Here, the visitors find all the possible kitchen utensils (knives, plates, containers and other ceramic items, wine rack, cheese covers, etc.), as well as a fully-equipped kitchen with cooker and embedded sinks.

Left and above
Natural oak "Vancouver" kitchen cabinets. The countertop (6cm thick) is made of Belgian blue stone.
A Smeg cooker. Accessories are from collections by Flamant.

This Flamant kitchen ("Vermont") is similarly in natural oak with a worktop in blue stone

(4cm thick). The cooker and hood are from Smeg.

LEFT AND ABOVE

"Vermont" kitchen in natural oak. 6cm thick countertop in Belgian blue stone.

ACHIEVEMENTS OF KITCHEN CREATORS | 113

These kitchens installed in the various Flamant establishments are especially inspiring and could serve as the starting point for an "à la carte" kitchen assembled according to the client's requirements. Flamant has a team of interior decoration consultants who is capable of providing professional advice when required.

LEFT AND ABOVE

This "Saint-Louis" kitchen from Flamant is painted in Flamant paints: Cabinets in Taupe (P.14) and wall in Balmoral Red (P.39). The countertop in Belgian blue stone has a thickness of 3cm. Cooker, hood and refrigerator are from Smeg. Accessories are from the Flamant collection.

ACHIEVEMENTS OF KITCHEN CREATORS | 115

CHAPTER II

INSPIRING KITCHENS

FRANCIS VAN DAMME:
THE CHARM OF YESTERDAY'S KITCHENS

Francis Van Damme is the master in restoration and rehabilitation of unique restoration materials patinated by time.

In these charming kitchens, past rich architectural traces are integrated: ancient cupboards of apothecaries, complete fittings of stores from the 19th century, wall cupboards, and wood-works found in the old Masters' Houses or from charming countrysidehomes, etc. This collection resembles the universe of a passionate broncantor where each piece would find itself a new life and meaning in the Francis Van Damme artisan joinery workshop in Wannegem-Lede.

Each of these five kitchens in this article relates a different history. They have, however, a trait in common: all these kitchens are fabricated according to the ancestral way of fabrication, and are so good that each one is unique. Like a virtuoso, Francis Van Damme knows how to adapt and transform his "findings" to create a kitchen that totally corresponds to the client's needs.

LEFT

This new construction is situated in a substantially timbered region. The initial aim was to create an abstemious kitchen, nonetheless, the charm of the countryside style strongly dominates the kitchen.

The ornaments above the chimney accord a French style to the room.

An old cupboard that used to be a wall in a school is now used as a cabinet to conceal kitchen electrical appliances.

The two old small door panels below the sink were once food cupboards.

A house situated in the residential green zone in the
Netherlands, immersed in the "Long Island" atmosphere,
is in need of a renovation. A solution was found to create a
space for this kitchen with a glass sliding partition slipped
within two walls. It has a two-door cupboard which comprises
a vapor furnace and a microwave oven. The kitchen was
integrated into one whole through the installation of a
glazed wall. The cabinets are painted in Holland White.

LEFT, ABOVE AND P. 126 TO 129

In the region of Lille, Francis Van Damme's French friends have renovated an extraordinary square farm. Installation of the kitchen was a challenge. The owners have chosen contemporary style appliances and kitchen accessories.

To enlarge the kitchen, a wall was demolished. The worktop was arranged around the centre pillar that was retained. The glass wall produces a "brewery" effect, which integrates culinary and gastronomical activities. To introduce light and to create a larger space effect, numerous glass windows and doors with square glass panels are used.

Francis Van Damme created this kitchen of an Antan style for an authentic house situated not too
far from Touquet. In Francis Van Damme's workshop, old shutters are transformed into cabinets. Door panels
of old windows are restored.

LEFT, ABOVE AND NEXT

A young couple was bold enough to renovate an old country house surrounded by a splendid park in an authentic way.

One of the old living rooms was transformed into the kitchen. During the renovation works, an old 18th century ceiling was revealed. The association of large windows and original floor provides a unique touch.

An old kitchen cabinet, an authentic La Cornue, was restored and equipped with modern elements. The glass windows were fabricated from oak windows from the 18th century with original glass panels retained.

THE MORIS GROUP: THE SOBRIETY AND RESERVE OF ANCIENT FLEMISH KITCHENS

Resistant to phenomena of trend and fashion, the Moris Group has remained loyal to the charm and beauty of ancient Flemish kitchens, equipped with modern comfort.

All the cupboards, doors and partitions are in solid wood and fabricated according to ancestral techniques by Bruno Van Winghe. The sinks, countertop, floors, wall coverings and chimneys lie in the hands of Guy Moris.

Nothing is left to chance. All the fabrication details, for example, the hinges, bolts and other hardware are similarly fabricated in the Moris workshop.

The "Flanders Architecture" department is lead by a team of passionate collaborators who have testified deep respect for our rich past architecture. Purity, simplicity and serenity inspire their projects which reflect the splendid interiors of the 17th and 18th centuries. Nevertheless, this style can be integrated into a very modern framework.

A COUNTRY-STYLE KITCHEN FROM POLYÈDRE

Henri-Charles Hermans, an antique dealer and decorator, has a workshop in England where he fabricates splendid kitchens in an artisanal way.

For his enterprise Polyédre, each kitchen project is a new creative challenge that relates to the client's universe and to suit the type of residential where the kitchen is integrated. This results in an interesting mix of old and new, which bridges timeless charm and modern functionality.

LEFT AND ABOVE

This country-style kitchen is fabricated in an artisanal way in the workshops of Polyédre.

The countertop is in blue stone.

THE ROMANTICISM KITCHENS
OF DOMINIQUE KOCH

Dominique Koch, a talented decorator, restored her house in Knokke-le-Zoute in 1997. In the past year in the same region, she has also realised scores of interior design projects with a common characteristic: all of them reveal their romanticism, her taste for ancient things and her respect for skilled techniques.

Most of the time, Dominique Koch also manages complete interior renovation projects even though she confessed that she has a preference for the creation and realisation of kitchens, which to her, is perceived as the heart of a dwelling.

LEFT AND OPPOSITE

Dominique Loch has designed and restored this kitchen in a typical fisherman's house in Zoute. Three small rooms are transformed into a deep kitchen that opens into nature.

The reddish ceramic floor tile comes from Bretagne. They are brighter tints and are perfectly coordinated with the color of the Aga kitchens.

The kitchen cabinets in MDF are painted in beige. The worktop is in aged Massangis stone.
Caramel slates cover the wall above the cooker.

The door on the left shown on the background of P.146 leads to this room where Dominique

Koch has decided to situate a wine cellar. Same ceramic floor tiles from

Bretagne are used.

Dominique Koch has created this spacious kitchen finished in natural oak, as well as the dining room in a restored Polders farm near Damse Vaart. The kitchen wall is entirely covered by cherry colour slates, which displays a marvelous contrast with the surrounding meadows. These greenish red tints are taken from the curtains made in the workshops of Zoute Nostalgie. The countertop is in Buxy stone; cooker is from La Cornue.

FROM KITCHEN TO COMPLETE INTERIOR DESIGN, THE VERSION OF SAND'S COMPANY

Not too long ago, the architectural firm HC Demyttenaere extended his sphere of activities to interior design and installation, and created in this field a distinct culture known as Sand's Company. The Sand's Company was established as a subsidiary wing under Demyttenaere's architectural firm in Knokke-Heist.

Sand's Company creates, executes and coordinates the interior design projects: panelling, dressing-rooms, libraries, and other custom-made works, for example, bathrooms, kitchens, consultations service on colour matters, etc.

The photographs on this page illustrate one of the first works from the conception office: a current and sober kitchen that is constituted of natural warm materials in a villa in Knokke-le-Zoute.

An American fridge by Amana.

In this kitchen, English sandstone is chosen for the floor finish; the wall tiles are from Dominique Desimpel. The kitchen cabinets integrated with a Smeg cooker are in painted MDF.

LEFT

The dining room ceiling is entirely covered in white painted timber boards.
Tables and benches are in solid oak, floor is in non-treated pine.

MONASTIC AMBIENCE OF ARCHITECT STEPHANE BOENS

Architect Stéphane Boens has conceived this bare-style kitchen for a country house. The warm materials, monochromatic palette of colours and the lighting effect create a refined and peaceful living place.

LEFT, ABOVE AND NEXT

This serene kitchen is equipped with an Aga cooker.

Wall tiles are from Dominique Desimpel.

ABOVE
The floor in natural
stones is selected from
Deknock in Zedelgem.

LEFT
The countertop is in white
Carrare marble.

The logical utilisation of natural materials and a sober palette of color tones produce a serene ambience, which is almost monastic.

RENOVATION OF AN ANCIENT DAIRY
BY ARCHITECT BERNARD DE CLERCK

Architect Bernard de Clerck has
transformed an old dairy into a
current dwelling, which by the
choice of natural materials and
integration of old elements, seems
to carry forward an impression of
sobriety with a classy and timeless
quality.

The kitchen in this house is a
beautiful illustration of art where
Architect De Clerck plays with
space, lighting and perspectives.

P. 162-163
The centre piece of
furniture, formerly an
ancient laboratory table,
is made of white volcanic
stone.

P. 164-165
The dining table was
installed on-site in the
old dairy. The floor is
in whitewashed oak.
Full-height cupboards
on the right of the photo
are from the 18th
century. Tables and
chairs are from Polyédre.

LEFT AND ABOVE
Several rooms are joined and transformed into one huge kitchen by Bernard De Clerck. The floor in checkered
patterns is formed by two types of natural stones. The same grey stone is used for the worktop. Visible above the
Lacanche cooker on the wall are the true petits blancs white tiles from Delft. The furniture is painted in grey
tones whereas warm colour tones are used for the walls.

A TIMELESS KITCHEN IN
A VILLA IN ZOUTE

All the kitchen installations of Luc Lormans (De Menagerie) are characterised by sober and pure lines without falling into the phenomenal trend of minimalism (see P. 16-29). The use of natural authentic materials gives his kitchens a warm ambience. This kitchen, in a villa from Zoute, is a very good example.

LEFT AND ABOVE

De Menagerie created this timeless kitchen for a villa situated in Knokke-Zoute. The cooker is from Lacanche.

CHAPTER III

EXCLUSIVE COOKERS AND ELECTRICAL HOUSEHOLD APPLIANCES

ADEK: UP-MARKET COOKERS AND ELECTRICAL HOUSEHOLD APPLIANCES

The Gantese enterprise Adek was founded in 1980 and has acquired, over 20 years, a solid reputation as a distributor of cookers and other exclusive kitchen appliances.

The choice in the up-market industry is large: quality cookers of La Cornue, Lacanche, Delaubrac, Godin, Viking, Mercury, Heartland, Metal Industries Lyon, Rosières, Smeg, etc; branded beautiful kitchen electrical appliances, refrigerators and wine racks (Sub Zero, La Glacière, Prizzon, Lumilandia, Amana, Liebherr, Eurocave); powerful yet silent hoods that can be made-to-measure, etc. Recently, Adek has showcased a pre-launch of a new product in Benelux: a corner refrigerator from Norcool, a Norwegian fabricator (www.norcool.com). It can be integrated in all kitchen types and is available in 120cm wide and 70cm deep.

LEFT AND ABOVE

Château 120, a La Cornue cooker in black nickel. A "bottom-mount" refrigerator from Sub Zero (model: 650S). A steel custom-made hood.

In Adek, the client gets complete and precise information. We could even find unique appliances in this Gantese distributor, which unfortunately, are not displayed in the retail shops.

Anxious to preserve its independence with respect to the brands and to offer new products permanently, Adek guarantees the client a choice that caters to individual needs. It is evident that Adek collaborates closely with the architects, decorators and kitchen designers to provide a service that includes consultations, installation and optimal service for the customer.

<small>LEFT AND ABOVE</small>

A Delaubrac Provencal 1600 cooker in black chrome consists of a gas oven, a small electric oven and a heating cupboard. It is the work of Costermans Villabouw.

A Prizzon refrigerator - Linea Fiftie in steel with glass viewing panels on the doors.

LEFT AND ABOVE

A Morice cooker – Suprême 130 in black brass.

A Mercury cooker (www.mercury-appliances.co.uk) in black steel and aluminium : a timeless model from the famous English designer, Seymour & Powell, which can be integrated into all kitchen types.

A steel "bottom-mount" refrigerator from Fisher & Paykel.

Left

A Lacanche cooker and a custom-made hood. The kitchen is designed by architect Bernard De Clerck.

BOS: DUTCH IMPORTER OF EXCLUSIVE UP-MARKET COOKERS

Bos Fornuizen is the Dutch distributor of exclusive up-market cookers like Aga, La Cornue, Godin, Molteni and Lacanche.

The enterprise is lead by Mr. and Mrs. Bos, with the assistance of their two sons and over ten collaborators.

BOS aims to guarantee the pleasure these exclusive cookers procures. All appliances are installed by their own engineering department. The chief installer, and three other installers not only install, but also provide maintenance service even if the cookers are bought from the retailers.

A visit to the large BOS showroom is worth the trip. Part of the showroom exclusively features Aga products. Weekly demonstrations are organised there.

Aga Classic "Special Edition" cooker.
It comes with two or four ovens.

Aga cooker: an assured value.

The new "Six Four" series of Aga.

LEFT AND ABOVE
Aga four ovens cooker in "British Racing Green" colour.

The model "Fontenay" with Lacanche fryer.

Lacanche cookers exist in several versions. Featured here is the version in stainless steel.

The "Souveraine" (110cm width) from Godin.

The top model of La Cornue.

"The Petit Château" from La Cornue exists in 60cm and 70cm widths.

"Cornuchef" from La Cornue.

Molteni: High-range Italian cooker.

ABEL FALISSE: EXPERIENCE, SAVOIR-FAIRE AND FIDELITY

Abel Falisse is the exclusive importer of "Viking" for Belgium and "Lacanche" and "Westahl" for Belgium and Luxembourg. The enterprise from Liège also carries their own brands like "Falis's", "Maxmatic" grinders, "Galvamet" hoods, "Suter" and "Aquastyl" sinks, "Arwa" taps, etc.

The family business founded in 1958 is currently led by two brothers, Jacques and Michel Falisse, and assisted by a new active generation. Not only are they one of the pioneers of culinary events in the Batibouw showroom for more than one century, they are one of the better distributors for up-market kitchen appliances. Their success is based on three principles: experience, savoir-faire and fidelity to the customer.

Thanks to "Viking", the enterprise is able to retain its reputation as Kitchens' Chief. Equipped with exceptional characteristics and performance, the "Viking" kitchen appliances represent the top range in the gastronomical cooking affair.

A Viking cooker in a kitchen designed by De Menagerie.

LEFT
An A'form kitchen with a Viking cooker.
The Viking range is available in 14 different colours.

A Lacanche cooker was chosen for this kitchen, which was created by Francis Van Damme.

This Westahl cooker in a Frank Tack project is the recent version of the legendary Lacanche kitchen. It has been in fabrication since the 18th century.

The factory of "Lacanche", situated in the village of LACANCHE in Bourgogne, fabricates furnaces since the 18th century. Specialising in the fabrication of professional cookers, it has developed the current "Lacanche" range for more than ten years in a timeless style, and has recently launched a new range, "Westahl", in a more modern style to adapt to the contemporary kitchens.

Recently, les Et. Falisse offers fabrication of appliances under the brand "Falis's", such as vitro-ceramics cooking surfaces, wok, teppanyaki, fryer, grill, domino gas and the revolutionary Aeraplan: an effective ventilation technique that draws out all odours and vapours towards a lower level before discharging them outside. This system allows the stove to be placed in front of the window or to maintain an unobstructed view with the cooking area on an island counter. As for traditional hoods, Falisse exclusively distributes "Galvamet" range.

LEFT
Lacanche cooker in a Polyedère kitchen.

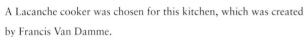

A classical conception: the Sintesi stainless steel furnace from Falis's offers nine functions.

The stove PAC90, with its four fires and its wok, offers a surface equal to a 90cm cooker. Above the stove is a professional mural hood of 120cm width: Galvamet GVY16.

From left to right: a deep fryer, the Aéraplan exhaust system with a 3-speed control, a stove of 70cm width, the Aéraplan without control button and an electric grill.

The Falis's furnace meets the most stringent high-quality criteria. The one above: AX30 (36 litres capacity) with a two-level hot air, grill and drying oven. The one below: RX60 (54 litres capacity) with nine functions. A Galvamet GVY17 hood.

The Aéraplan table hood, thanks to its flexibility, allows the utilisation of gas wok combined with, for example, a two-fire vitro-ceramic stove CI12.

CHAPTER IV

CHOICE OF MATERIALS
IN THE KITCHEN

THE CRAFTSMAN TILE OF DOMINIQUE DESIMPEL

Dominique Desimpel nourishes a passion for craft-design tiles and exceptional natural stones that give the final touch to a kitchen.

In his Knokke business, Dominique Desimpel presents the most beautiful manually fabricated floor and wall tiles: enamel terracotta manually coloured in various tints of whites and beiges, marble mosaic wall tiles all fabricated by hand, authentic Moroccan slates, etc.

The timeless and unique characteristics of these manually fabricated tiles are a more important feature than their originals.

Demanding clients, renowned interior architects and acclaimed kitchen designers dismiss industrial and impersonal characteristics of machine-made tiles. They prefer tiles with a poetic touch and savoir-faire craftsmanship.

ABOVE AND NEXT
A kitchen by De Menagerie.

LEFT
Craft-design tiles by Dominique Desimpel are installed in this kitchen that is designed by architect Stéphane Boens.

P. 196-197

The tiles of Dominique Desimpel are similarly used in this
De Menagerie kitchen.

LOUIS CULOT:
NATURAL STONE IN THE KITCHEN

For three generations, Louis Culot's reputation has grown to be one of the best enterprises in Benelux that specialises in natural stone. It is capable of providing highly recognised professional works to clients.

The use of natural stone in the kitchen is Louis Culot's specialty: for countertops (for this purpose, the enterprise has bought 2 machines with CNC point), as well as for floor and wall finishes. Numerous renowned culinary specialists have chosen this company own by Londerzeel for its excellent service, its fast delivery period (within a week), the finish quality and its competitive prices. Apart from dealing with the specialists, Louis Culot sells to individuals as well. It is definitely worth the trip to the enterprise's showroom. At the showrooms, the clients would discover diverse marvellous kitchens.

LEFT AND ABOVE

All wall and floor finishes are supplied and installed with Louis Culot using Kashmir White polished granite. The countertop is designed by a Louis Culot kitchen designer and milled by one of the company's machines: a process that guarantees a perfect finish.

These extremely thick countertops (8cm) are produced by
Louis Culot in Belfast black granite "Noir de Marlin"
with a choice of a softened finish.

This kitchen shows a harmony of red and grey tones. The countertop (8cm thick) is made of Rojo Eros Silestone: a Spanish stone composite that is extremely durable and has grown in popularity.
The walls are painted in the same red tone.

In 2003, Louise Culot completed over 30 projects each week: with a variety of natural stones (granite, Belgian blue stone, Azul Cascais, Buxy, etc.), and Spanish composite stone, Silestone, which is now frequently used. Therefore Louis Culot always maintains extra stock of the six most popular colours. This stone is very durable and easy to maintain which are important assets in modern kitchens.

During the last years, Louis Culot appreciated the elements of a strong growth: the enterprise constantly relies on more than 20 motivated collaborators. Two teams are permanently involved in the design of kitchen layouts and recently, an interior designer was employed to generate form as dreamed by the client from a natural stone.

LEROU: HARDWARE RESTORATION AND EXCLUSIVE VALVES AND FITTINGS

Lerou Ijzerwaren, one of the oldest enterprises in Belgium, was founded in 1792. The enterprise specialises in ironmongery – particularly on door, furniture and restoration accessories, security hardware and exclusive kitchen, bathrooms and wardrobes accessories.

The assortment is particularly vast and they are assembled in a large building in the industrial zone in Bruges.

The emphasis is placed on ironmongery of exclusive restorations and on the craftsmanship fabrication. The enterprise, as a result, is frequently employed by interiors designers, restorers and carpenters who perpetuate the tradition of craft-design trade. Individuals too, can approach Lerou. One of Lerou's largest assets is the huge range of finishes adapted to meet client's taste including bronze, nickel chrome, silver and gold.

In addition, Lerou carries their own range of patinas: Sylt, Cowes and Rétaise. The enterprise proposes conjoint ironmongeries of top quality for furniture and on doors to the bathroom for handles, latches and locks.

LEFT AND ABOVE

Lerou is one of the most famous Belgian distributors of restoration hardware, valves and fittings in wrought iron and massive brass.

An old Crémone
des Ardennes

P. 204-205

Lerou's restoration hardware is a duplicate
of very old models.

Handles in "Rétaise" finish.

Recommended reading

- Martin Edic & Richard Edic, "Kitchens that work. The practical guide to creating a great kitchen". The Taunton Press, 1997.
- Anthony Rowley, "Le livre de la cuisine". Flammarion, Parijs, 1999.
- Terence Conran & Victoria Davis, "Terence Conran on Restaurants". Conran Octopus, 2000.
- "Easy Living". Conran Octopus Limited, 1999.
- "Cooking". Alfred A. Knopf, 1995.
- Fran Warde, "Eat drink live". Ryland, Peters & Small, 2000.
- Alice King, "Fabulous Fizz". Ryland, Peters & Small.
- Juliet Harbutt, "The World Encyclopedia of Cheese". Lorenz Books.
- Elisabeth David, "Mediterranean Food". Penguin Books.
- Elisabeth David, "French Provincial Cooking". Penguin Books, 1964.
- Donna Hay, "The New Cook". Murdoch Books, 1997.
- Donna Hay, "Entertaining". Murdoch Books, 1998.
- "Invitation, le monde de Gunther Lambert". Thormann & Goetsch.
- Gunther Lambert, "Recipes for Living and Dining".
- Fred Bridge & Jean F. Tibbetts, "The Well-Tooled Kitchen". Hearst Books, 1991.
- Kim Johnson Gross & Jeff Stone, "Cooking Tools". Thames and Hudson, 1996.
- Joël Robuchon & Patricia Wells, "Le meilleur et le plus simple de Robuchon". Robert Laffont, 1994.
- "Les dimanches de Joël Robuchon". Chêne, 1993.
- Roger Vergé, "Les légumes de mon moulin". Flammarion, 1992.
- Georgeanne Brennan, "Saveurs du Potager". Flammarion, 1994.
- Jane Sigal, "La Normandie". Hatier, 1993.
- Linda Collister, "Morning Bakes". Ryland, Peters & Small, 2000.
- Annie Nichols, "Potatoes: From Gnocchi to Mash". Ryland, Peters & Small.
- Fiona Beckett, "Wine by Style". Mitchell Beazley.
- Rory Ross, "The Gastrodome Cookbook". Pavillion, 1995.
- "Gordon Ramsay's Passion for Flavour". Conran Octopus, 1996.
- Raymond Blanc, "Blanc vite: Fast Fresh Food".
- Georges Blanc, "De la vigne à l'assiette". Hachette, 1995.
- James Turnbull, "La cave et le vin". Editions Eyrolles, 1995.
- Florine Boucher, Kees Hageman, "Bijzondere recepten van Mario". De Toorts.
- Jeffrey Steingarten, "The man who ate everything".
- Serge Dansereau, "Food & Friends".

P. 210-211
This kitchen was designed by Polyèdre.

PHOTOGRAPHY CREDITS

All photographs : Jo Pauwels, with exception of the following :